MR. HUMBL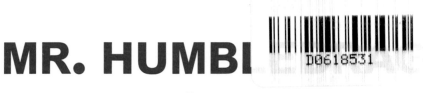

by Dan Zevin

Illustrated by Dylan Klymenko

 THREE RIVERS PRESS
NEW YORK

Mr. Humblebrag wanted to make the whole wide world happy.

Happy for *him*!

With piles of money and loads of success, he couldn't help but to broadcast how #blessed he was.

And he tried extra hard to act bashful, not boastful.

WORK
4 FOOD

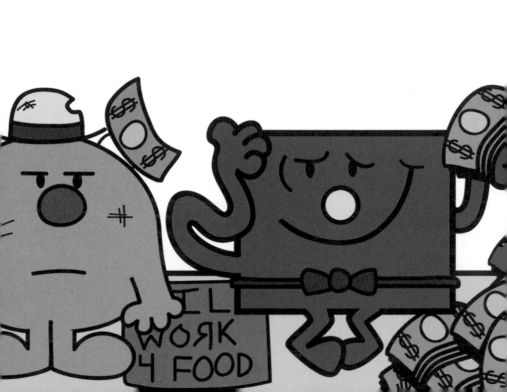

"Everybody loves a winner, as long as he acts like a loser," Mr. Humblebrag liked to say. "Jeez, how did a dummy like me ever figure *that* one out?"

One day, Mr. Humblebrag was on a tropical cruise vacation while everyone else was at their soul-crushing, dead-end jobs.

He was sure they'd feel better if they only knew what a fun time he was having on the lido deck.

"But what if they resent your ceaseless good fortune?" asked his fiancée, Little Miss Porn Star.

"Not a problem!" he replied. "I will do the thing where I make them feel sorry for me."

Gleefully, he posted a photo of them sipping papaya coladas in the pool.

Uh-oh, does that look like bragging?

Don't worry, here comes the humble. . . .

"Leave it to me to twist my ankle doing the limbo!" he false-modestly wrote. "Now I have to stay off my feet for the rest of the week!"

Just then, a comment appeared in his feed.

It was from his coworker, Mr. Snark!

"I feel your pain," it said.

Mr. Humblebrag felt validated inside.

Because he didn't understand sarcasm.

One day, Mr. Humblebrag dipped into his trust fund.

He bought a shiny new Tesla.

"It cost a katrillion dollars and a bazillion cents," he was embarrassed to tell his five million Friends. "So if anyone can bail me out of debtors' prison, I'd be #grateful because I'm #poor!"

AT&T
Status

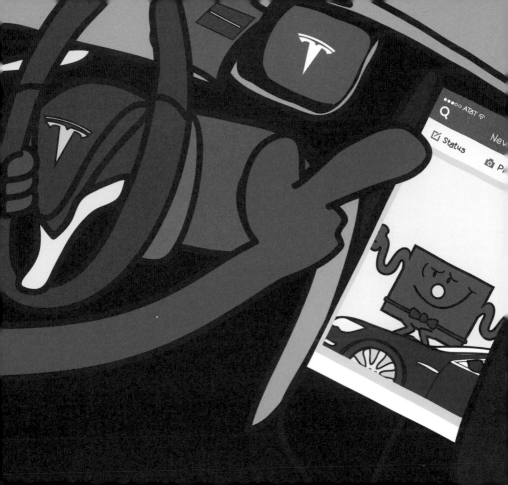

Mr. Humblebrag couldn't wait to customize his car.

First, he put a subtle decal on the back window, identifying the small college outside of Boston he attended.

Now he wouldn't have to tell everyone where he went to school.

Because that would sound snobby, wouldn't it?

H

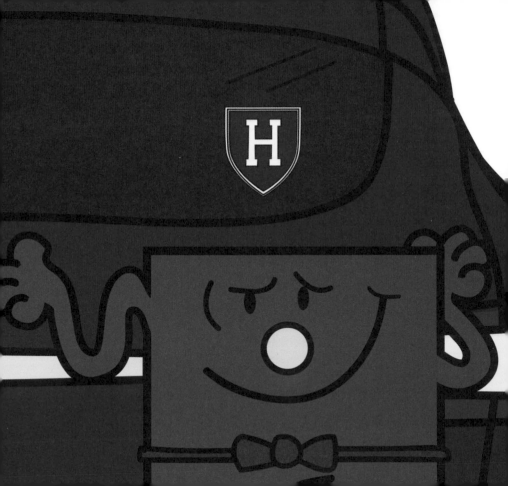

Soon, he discovered his favorite standard feature.

Can you guess what it was?

The horn!

He'd toot it in the morning,
he'd toot it in the afternoon,
he'd toot it all night long.

He sure liked tooting his own horn!

Toot
Toot

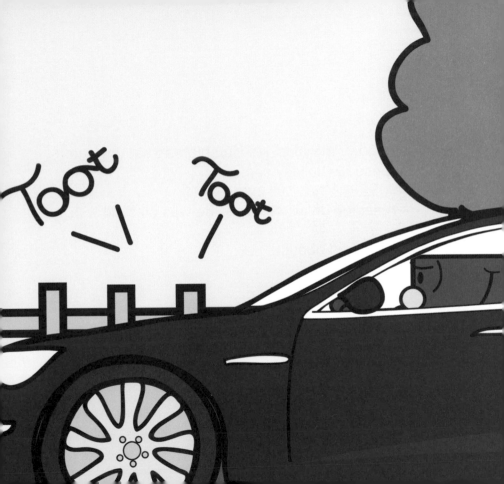

One snowy morning, Mr. Humblebrag sat down to compose his holiday card.

He reflected on all the things he was blessed with.

And honored about.

And thankful for.

And, especially, humbled by.

Like his movie deal!

And his TED Talk!

And his Ironman race!

And his transformational trip to the African village where he saw the endangered turtles and met the malnourished orphans.

Not to mention his upcoming cover shoot for the Abercrombie & Fitch catalogue.

"Guess they somehow mixed me up with a dude who looks like an Abercrombie & Fitch model," he humorously joked.

He sure was self-deprecating instead of self-promoting!

Later, Mr. Humblebrag was flabbergasted.

He'd been nominated for Humblebragger of the Year by the Academy of Humblebragging Arts and Sciences!

Of course, he was too modest to go around telling everyone about it.

So he asked his mother to do it instead.

She loved humblebragging about her children.

She was doing it before it was even a thing!

"My baby boy is being flown first class to Hollywood!" she faxed all her friends. "Proud to have provided him with my DNA."

When they announced his name as the winner, Mr. Humblebrag looked astonished, amazed, and all agog.

Practicing in front of the mirror all day really paid off!

"Golly, I did not write a speech, since I believed I would lose," he said pseudo-sincerely.

Then he spent forty-five minutes thanking those who believed in him though he did not believe in himself.

Such as Mr. Zuckerberg, Mr. Snoop Dogg, and Little Miss Malala.

#BLESSED

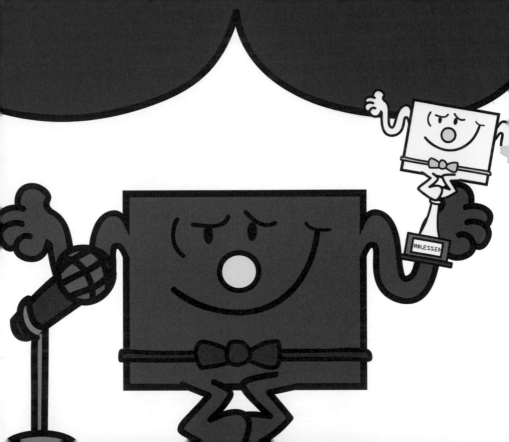

When he went to bed that night, Mr. Humblebrag felt #unworthy.

You see, he was too modest to think he deserved that award.

And too generous to keep it all for himself.

So can you guess what he did so no one felt left out?

He shared it!

On Twitter, Facebook, Instagram, Google+, Pinterest, and Snapchat.

THREE RIVERS PRESS and the Tugboat design are registered trademarks of
Penguin Random House LLC.

Library of Congress Cataloging-in-Publication Data is available upon request.

ISBN 978-1-101-90446-6
eBook ISBN 978-1-101-90458-9

PRINTED IN CHINA

Illustrations by Dylan Klymenko
Cover design by Dylan Klymenko

10 9 8 7 6 5 4 3 2 1

First Edition